The History of Medieval Philosophy

UNI SLOVAKIA series
Volume 8

The History of Medieval Philosophy
Selected Figures of Scholastic Tradition I

Ladislav Tkáčik

Bibliographic Information published by the Deutsche Nationalbibliothek

The Deutsche Nationalbibliothek lists this publication in the Deutsche
Nationalbibliografie; detailed bibliographic data is available in the internet at http://dnb.d-nb.de

The publication of this book is part of the project Support for Improving the Quality
of Trnava University (ITMS code 26110230092) — preparation of a Liberal Arts study
program, which was supported by the European Union via its European Social Fund and
by the Slovak Ministry of Education within the Operating Program Education. The text
was prepared at the Department of Philosophy, Faculty of Philosophy, Trnava University
in Trnava.

Design and Layout: © Jana Sapáková, Layout JS.
Printing: VEDA, Publishing House of the Slovak Academy of Sciences

ISSN 2366-2697
ISBN 978-3-631-67460-4
E-ISBN 978-3-653-06646-3
DOI 10.3726/978-3-653-06646-3

© Peter Lang GmbH
Internationaler Verlag der Wissenschaften
Frankfurt am Main 2016

All rights reserved.

Peter Lang Edition is an Imprint of Peter Lang GmbH.
Peter Lang – Frankfurt am Main · Bern · Bruxelles · New York · Oxford · Warszawa · Wien

All parts of this publication are protected by copyright. Any utilisation outside the
strict limits of the copyright law, without the permission of the publisher, is forbidden
and liable to prosecution. This applies in particular to reproductions, translations,
microfilming, and storage and processing in electronic retrieval systems.

This publication has been peer reviewed.

Printed in Slovakia

www.peterlang.com

Contents

1. Boundaries and Concept of Middle Ages and its Philosophical Thinking 7
2. Anicius Manlius Severinus Torquatus Boethius 19
3. Pseudo-Dionysius the Areopagite 29
4. Carolingian Renaissance 39
5. Johannes Scotus Eriugena 45
6. Anselm of Canterbury 61
7. Peter Abelard 71
8. Albertus Magnus and Thomas Aquinas 89

Used and Recommended Literature 99

1. Boundaries and Concepts of the Middle Ages and its Philosophical Thinking

Claudio Leonardi says that the "Middle Ages represent a historic period, in which the identity, which was denied and destroyed by the modern world and which however is now being discovered again in its beauty, was established. It is a period in which dialogue and therefore also a conflict between faith and intellect, church and empire and between culture based in God and culture based in man, were possible. It is a living space in which mystique and philosophy could exist side by side on a historic level. It is world which is lost today and which we can get hold of again only by intellectual appropriation" (*Středověká Latinská Literatura*, p. 24).

To understand the specificity of certain period and conceive its essence, it is undoubtedly desirable to distinguish it from the times which preceded and follow it. This belief lies behind our effort to periodise time. This effort, which no longer has theological and eschatological characteristics, can be traced back to the 14th and 15th centuries. It was during this period when the epoch of the Middle Ages was defined for the first time. Therefore, in the sense of more modern periodization, the Middle Ages were defined as the first epoch.

Medieval scholars restricted the term "ancient times" or "antiquity" to the epoch of Greek and Roman erudition, which they tried to continue. The term "antiquity" in the sense of an epoch which precedes the Middle Ages can be found already in work of Michel Eyquem de Montaigne (1533 – 1592) from the year 1581 and in the plural it can be found in work of cardinal and diplomat Jean du Bellay (1493 – 1560) *Antiquités de Rome (1558)*.

The word and the notion of the "Middle Ages" can be found in the 14th century in work of Italian humanists, among whom a sense of new times, which were necessary to be distinguished from the fading epoch, started to prevail. It was this feeling – which they devised themselves – which led to a pejorative definition of the Middle Ages. They defined its beginning roughly by the fall of Roman Empire and termed it "media aetas" (middle age). Probably the first note of this kind can be found in the work of Italian poet Francesco Petrarca (1304 – 1374). Papal librarian Giovanni Andrea (1417 – 1475) already used the term "Middle Ages" in the sense of chronological periodization when he used it to distinguish medieval authors from modern ones.

However the term "Middle Ages" started to be used more generally only among scholars at the end of 17th century. The distinction between medieval and antiquity can be found in the dictionary *Glossarium Mediae et Infimae Latinitatis* (1678) of Charles du Fresne and in the second volume of *Historia Universalis* (1698) by Christoph Keller who defined the Middle Ages by the reign of emperor Constantine and the conquest of Constantinople by Turks in 1453. This periodization was later adopted by the philosophers of the 18th century.

To call an epoch middle age, mid-times, means to deny a name to it and therefore it already involves some sort of judgement. To consider a time which would just bridge the antique as valuable on its own and time which aspires to revive the antique means to understand the Middle Ages as a perplexed intermezzo at best, an interval, as a waiting period for the new epoch which will revive the Greek-Roman ancient times and antiquity. In between there was nothing, specifically there was nothing that would be worth reviving. Only the renaissance supposedly revives the ancient times.

Among 17th and 18th century authors, the general term "Middle Ages" had a spirit of judgement or dislike, not dissimilar to the more narrow term "gothic", which was a synonym for ugly and barbarian from a renaissance perspective. Like their refusal of gothic "primitivism", the renaissance also loathed medieval philosophy because of its Arabic influence. It is the judging of theology, philosophy and science of the Middle Ages that dominated the scientific discourse for quite a long time. In his *Vorlesungen über die Philosophie der Weltgeschichte* published after his death, Georg Wilhelm Friedrich Hegel (1770 – 1831) recommended his students wear imaginary seven-league boots when studying history of philosophy in order to get through the period between the 6th and 16th century as fast as possible. A student who is getting to Descartes should, according to Hegel, call out "Land ho!" in relief like a sailor.

Paradoxically however, in Hegel's times, the Middle Ages were idealised among the romantics. Romantics admired the Middle Ages and began to study it with enthusiasm. In the Middle Ages, they saw some sort of childhood of nations, which transformed into adulthood during the renaissance. A vivid interest in the Middle Ages was shown by scholars and artists of the 19th century. The influence of the publication of "The Hunchback of Notre Dame" (1821) by Victor Hugo or "William Tell" by Richard Wagner has to be mentioned in this respect. The establishment of the *École National des Chartres* in 1821 in France, the establishment of the German edition of the primary sources *Monumenta Germaniae Historica* in 1819 or the establishment of the historic French school *Annales* in 20th century had a great importance for study of the Middle Ages. It is possible to say that the intensity of interest in the Middle Ages grew significantly in 20th century and today interest in this remarkable yet overlooked and generalised period of human history, prevails.

To more or less know a continuous period means to recognise its particularity. To recognise the Middle Ages, therefore, also means to conceive its boundaries and its detachedness from the preceding and following periods. What could then be the beginning and end of medieval philosophy? As mentioned above, Keller defines the Middle Ages by the constitution of Constantinople in 330 and its fall in 1453. The traditional definition links the beginning of the Middle Ages to the end of Western Roman Empire in 476 and the dethronement of (roughly) fifteen year old Roman Emperor Romulus Augustulus by a Germanic army-leader Odoacer. Its end is linked to conquest of Constantinople by Ottoman Turks in 1453, or to the year 1492 when Christopher Columbus discovered Americas.

We cannot understand the beginning of the Middle Ages as a certain moment. However, from the point of view of philosophy, there is one symbolic date. Hegel used to talk about it as the end of institutions of pagan philosophy. It is the year 529 in which the Platonian Academy in Athens, which had existed for nine centuries, was closed by the act of Emperor Justinian (482 – 565). Moreover, in the same year, Benedict of Nursia (480

– 543/547) founded a Benedictine abbey in the Monte Cassino mountains. Therefore, it is an appropriate date in which two symbolic events occurred: something old finished, something that characterised antique scholarship, and something new started;, something that would determine the whole of medieval Europe. At the same time, the change of stage was also being finished and the contrast between the new and the old is indubitable.

What was Justinian's period like? Thanks to him, the supremacy of Byzantine Rome was reaffirmed and Constantin's empire was reunited. Obviously, the political power of empire could not tolerate a pagan institution such as the Platonian academy on its territory and it decided to close it down. The academy used to explicitly oppose the ever more dominant Christianity. In this respect, the script *Katá Christianṓn* (Against the Christians) of its representative Porphyry of Tyre (233 – 301/305) can be cited as an example. After its closure, most of the members of academy found refuge in the near East, mostly in Persia where they were favoured by the ruling dynasty of Sasans.

Paganism was fading out and Christianity was establishing itself. In what sense could the contemporary people perceive this rupture? How radical was it? Surely, it was a more radical difference than the differences between the antique philosophical schools, for example between the Ionian natural philosophy and Socrates. The transition from Plato to Origen was much more radical. The key to understanding this shift is the realisation of the radicalness of the fundamental event of Christianity – the event of *incarnation*. It was an event which, in its meaning, was more significant than the fall of Alexandrian empire or the collapse of the Roman Empire. From the Christian point of view, the event of incarnation completely revolutionised the consideration of the meaning of history, of reality as a whole and of the meaning of individual human existence. It was not about developing the antique drafts and intuitions anymore, this was a radically new era. One cannot understand the Middle Ages without taking this Christian perspective into consideration. It is fundamentally present in the thinking of medieval scholars. The belief that truth and meaning are accessible to humankind in the historic person of Christ naturally transformed not only theology but also philosophy.

At the same time, we cannot date the beginning of the Middle Ages from the antique Christian authors such as Justin, Clement of Alexandria or Augustine. Augustine (354 – 430) still lived in the Roman Empire, in the world of Hellenism and Neoplatonism. Rome was still the symbol of world order. Only the shock caused by the conquest of Rome in the year 410 by Alaric brought Augustine to the concept of "God's community". Augustine died during the siege of his residential pontifical city of Hippo by vandals and thus his life ended symbolically straddling the old and the new. His work also shows that he was still a person of antique times but at the same time he anticipated many of the themes of medieval philosophy and theology.

The Roman Empire was flooded by new nations that invaded the original antique space from the north and settled there. Gradually, during the Middle Ages, the cultural centres moved from Rome, Athens, Alexandria, Atiochia and Carthage to Theodoric's court, Ravenna, Verona, Pavia, the court of Charlemagne in Aachen, Canterbury, Oxford, Paris and Cologne... Metaphorically, we could describe this process as settling into an old occupied house. This perspective can help us to understand the nature of medieval philosophy which is incongruent at the beginning. Medieval philosophy is significantly influenced by the disunity of the world. New nations adopt old thinking, new languages and new cultures.

Of course, it is simpler to identify the beginning of the Middle Ages than its end. The boundary continuously shifts just like our perspectives. It is possible to say that with the Middle Ages a new period of world history began, however this period did not end with the Middle Ages. As Le Goff says, the medieval nature of thinking is not lost in the modern times. Its Christian element is not lost either, and it is also impossible to discuss a rupture between the Middle Ages and the Renaissance...

The translocation of the centres mentioned above can be characterised more precisely as so called *translatio studiorum*" as a translocation of the study centres which was related to the translocation of the political and cultural centres. For example, in the period of Carolingian Renaissance, Alcuin talks about the creation of new philosophical Athens in France. Or when an argument breaks out between the law faculty of a Paris university and the canonry of Notre-Dame in 1384, the lawyers defend themselves using the following logic: after all, they were the oldest study centre in the world which just moved from Athens to Rome and from Rome to Paris. Similarly, in 1405, chancellor of the university Jean Gerson (1363 – 1429) includes Charles VI in a preachment concerning a lineage of rule which spans from Athens through Rome to Paris. According to him, the tradition of knowledge develops analogically: from Jews through to Egyptians to Paris. We can perceive the regression of pagan centres in a similar way: Athens moved to Persia, from Persia to Harran and Alexandria and from Alexandria to Baghdad. Similar translocations characterise the whole early Middle Ages and they offer a historical framework for the whole turbulent epoch.

This perspective translated itself into the basic characteristics of medieval philosophy as well, into its *scholasticity* (i.e. its 'schoolness'). However this scholasticity has to be understood in a broader sense. It involves the adoption of the discovered tradition by new nations as well. And if this adoption of the old antique heritage and its adaptation was supposed to be effective, it had to be accompanied by a scholastic systematisation and classification. If the Middle Ages had not meet these requirements, we probably would not have any direct access to Plato or Aristotle today. The adoption of the great richness of antique thought and culture was accompanied by a great intellectual culture, creativity, independence, intellectual honesty and geniality of medieval scholars. The dark side of such a perception of scholasticity was exhaustion and unoriginality which were becoming ever more obvious towards the end of the Middle Ages. Medieval philosophy became increasingly overloaded by itself; it is confronted with new questions which require new answers, yet it kept revising the old. This of course led to sterility and decay. Medieval philosophy fell apart on its own from within: it exhausted itself.

However, we have to realise that there is no universal history of medieval philosophy and similarly there is no universal historical periodization. We have to distinguish between the development of Latin, Greek, Jewish, Arabic and Muslim worlds. People of the same period do not necessarily experience the same times. The times of separate cultures are not concurrent despite their interference. It is more appropriate to look at history as a plurality of centres and times as is indirectly testified by the use of different calendars and chronologies.

In this manner, a deconstruction of traditional and convenient judgements of the Middle Ages as "dark" is already completed in these preliminary thoughts. In the following chapters, this view will be elaborated. We will examine whether a truly original and new philosophical thinking existed in the Middle Ages; whether medieval philosophy can be simply interchanged with theology as is continually suggested, that is, was philosophy in the Middle Ages just *ancilla theologiae* (a servant of theology)?

2. Anicius Manlius Severinus Torquatus Boethius

Boethius (around 480 – 524/526) was born into a patrician family of Roman lineage in Anicius, from which Benedict of Nursia also came. He lived in times of epochal changes: in 476 Odoacer dethroned the last Western Roman Emperor Augustulus and in 493, he was defeated by Ostrogoth king Theodoric (453 – 526). In 529, four years after Boethius' death, the Platonian academy was closed down.

Boethius was raised as a Christian and in the tradition of classic Roman education. He also knew Greek which was no longer very common during this period. His unusual skills caught the attention of King Theodoric, who employed him in his court. Boethius held high state positions and became a consul at the age of 30 in 510, and rose to the position of *magister officiorum* in the year 520. His incorruptibility and fairness led to hostility among the members of Roman senate. Due to suspicions of an alliance with the Roman bishop John I, and suspicions of a supposed agreement with the Byzantine Empire, Theodoric had Boethius imprisoned and executed in 525 without a trial. As Theodoric was known as a judicious and merciful ruler, this action was never fully understood.

For scholastic philosophy, Boethius became an archetypal figure of almost paradigmatic significance. It is obvious that he lived on a border during a period of great transition, in some sort of early medieval "melting pot". His position was a chance, challenge, but at the same time, a large risk. From the Romans, he faced a risk of misunderstanding and the suspicion of collaboration and cultural betrayal to the barbarians. At the same time, as a catholic, he worked among Arian Goths who could suspect him for subversive intentions. However, despite his tragic fate, Boethius became more than a politically successful intermediary.

Many traditional historians of philosophy diminish his importance by saying that he never created any original system of thought. However, the importance of his work lies in the broad understanding of translating and commenting. Boethius prepared the basics of propaedeutics. Following the Augustinian study system *artes liberales* (as an opposition to *artes serviles*) he devoted himself to *quadrivium* and *trivium,* convinced that philosophy and theology need prior preparation of thinking (the 7 liberal arts consisted of: *quadrivium* or arithmetic, geometry, astronomy and music and *trivium* combined to make grammar, rhetoric and dialectics/logic). Boethius wrote the interpretation and introduction to quadrivium and by doing so he significantly contributed to the transplantation of the old erudition into the new world.

Around the year 510 Boethius reached a cultural conviction about the need for a translation of the entirety of both Plato's and Aristotle's work into Latin. He started with a translation of Porphyry's *Isagoge* and commented on it in five books. He translated Aristotle's *Categoriae* from *Organon* (set of writings on logic) and commented on them in *In Praedicamenta Aristotelis*. Then followed a translation of and commentary on Aristotle's writings on verbalisation, *Peri Hermeneias*. Around the year 514, he translated and commented on Aristotle's analytics and he wrote his interpretation of sophistic proofs. Among his theological writings which were created between the years 510 – 520 *Liber contra Eutychen et Nestorium, De Trinitate, De Hebdomadibus, De Fide Catholica* and *De Fide* can be mentioned.

Let's have a look at Boethius' thoughts about music: "Thus it follows that, since there are four mathematical disciplines, the others are concerned with the investigation of truth, whereas music is related not only to speculation but to morality as well. For nothing is more consistent with human nature than to be soothed by sweet modes and disturbed by their opposites. And this affective quality of music is not peculiar to certain professions or ages, but it is common to all professions; and infants, youths and old people as well are so naturally attuned to the musical modes by a certain spontaneous affection... soul of the universe is united by a musical concord (Plato Timaeus 37 A). For when we compare that which is coherently and harmoniously joined together in sound-that is, that which gives us pleasure-so we come to recognise that we ourselves are united according to this same principle of similarity. For similarity is pleasing, whereas dissimilarity is unpleasant and contrary. From this same principle radical changes in one's character also occur... Thus from all these examples it appears to be beyond doubt that music is so naturally a part of us that we cannot be without it, even if we so wished. For this reason the power of the mind ought to be directed toward fully understanding by knowledge what is inherent in us through nature. Thus just as erudite scholars are not satisfied by merely seeing colors and forms without also investigating their properties, so musicians should not be satisfied by merely finding pleasure in music without knowing by what musical proportions these sounds are put together" (*Principles of Music*, I, 1).

However, Boethius' most famous work is his script *Consolatio Philosophiae* (Consolation of Philosophy) which he wrote in prison waiting for his death. A peculiarity of this text is the absence of Christian ideas which, in combination with his existentially serious situation, led many historians to doubt his Christianity. The script in question is of a high literary quality and Boethius' rare personal characteristics clearly show throughout. It is a work dedicated to questions of theodicy in the context of theistic metaphysics. Philosophy is personified into an image of a beautiful woman who engages in a conversation about the meaning of hardship, suffering and injustice with Boethius. All events lead to good and bliss. Moral evil can only stem from a fallacy based on an inverted hierarchic order of values which changes high into low. The reason for this is some sort of metaphysical infatuation which prevents us from seeing the deeper connections. An obvious allusion to Augustine can be found here as well: Evil exists in the world so that the bad will be punished and made good, and so that the good ones can be tested and their goodness reaffirmed. Boethius defends the opinion that the only solution to the problem of life is to strive for good, i.e. a quest for what is represented by Philosophy. In philosophy, people connect to the divine and achieve consolation. Despite the absence of many Christian thought concepts, overall Boethius' thinking meets Christian tradition.

Let's mention at least several fragments here. Boethius describes his encounter with Philosophy with these words: "Accordingly, when I had lifted my eyes and fixed my gaze upon her, I beheld my nurse, Philosophy, whose halls I had frequented from my youth up. — 'Ah! why,' I cried, 'mistress of all excellence, hast thou come down from on high, and entered the solitude of this my exile? Is it that thou, too, even as I, mayst be persecuted with false accusations?' — 'Could I desert thee, child,' said she, 'and not lighten the burden which thou hast taken upon thee through the hatred of my name, by sharing this trouble? Even forgetting that it were not lawful for Philosophy to leave companionless the way of the innocent, should I, thinkest thou, fear to incur reproach, or shrink from it, as though some strange new thing had befallen? Thinkest thou that now, for the first time in an evil age, Wisdom hath been assailed by peril? Did I not often in days of old, before my servant Plato lived, wage stern warfare with the rashness of folly?" (I, 3) The text concludes with an apology of freedom: "... the freedom of man's will stands unshaken, and laws are not unrighteous, since their rewards and punishments are held forth to wills unbound by any necessity. God, who foreknoweth all things, still looks down from above, and the ever-present eternity of His vision concurs with the future character of all our acts, and dispenseth to the good rewards, to the bad punishments. Our hopes and prayers also are not fixed on God in vain, and when they are rightly directed cannot fail of effect. Therefore, withstand vice, practise virtue, lift up your souls to right hopes, offer humble prayers to Heaven. Great is the necessity of righteousness laid upon you if ye will not hide it from yourselves, seeing that all your actions are done before the eyes of a Judge who seeth all things." (V, 6).

The significance of Boethius' work for the whole Latin Middle Ages can be appropriately summarised in three titles which were ascribed to him by medieval scholars. They called him *master of translation* (*magister translationis*). However, in his case, the translation has to be understood as a form of cultural life itself and not just as a technical art. Boethius adapted basic Greek notional terminology for antiquity into Latin; he created notional and terminological bonds: *energeia* = *actus*; *dynamis* = *potentia*; *eidos*, idea = species; *arché* = *principium*; *symbebekos* = *accidens*; *res* = stoic term of reality. Similarly, he mediated the Platonian notions of God, bliss and ontological participation for the Middle Ages and he also attempted one of the first solutions of universals. Moreover, his translations of Aristotle were the only source of knowledge about him until the 13th century.

The second title ascribed to him by history is the title *master of choice* (*magister electionis*). Boethius was convinced about the fundamental agreement of Plato and Aristotle. Despite the fact that his ambition was to translate the complete works of both authors, he chose a very appropriate strategy. He started with the selection of the most significant texts for the future. In his work, the focus on the the philosophical tradition as a whole to avoid bias is apparent. He did not fall into the alluring trap of the choice of the 'right' opinion, knowing that his complicated contemporary context asked for mediation of *instrumentarium* of philosophical thinking rather than definite perspectives. He understood that a culture in danger needs inclusion ("also – also") rather than definite perception ("either – or"). It needs the preservation of a common thought and it profits more from synthesis than exclusion.

The third title given to Boethius was *master of definitions (magister definitionis)*. His philosophical definitions and quotations became so popular that their users no longer even bothered to state his name. Some of his most popular definitions were his definition of person as *"individua rationalis naturae substantia"* (an individual substance of a rational nature), his definition of eternity as a complete and perfect ownership of unlimited and never ending life, and his definition of knowledge as *"quidquid cognoscitur ad modum cognoscentis cognoscitur"* (everything we know is not perceived according to its nature but rather according to the abilities of the perceiving). The texts of Peter Abelard prove the importance of Boethius, as although written 600 years after his death, Boethius is mentioned on almost every page.

Let us examine the key themes of Boethius' work. How does Boethius understand God? For philosophical theology, God is a central problem. According to Boethius,

God is neither a person nor a *res*. God is a separate being *ipsum esse*, a pure form without matter, he is what he is, while everything else is not what it is. In accordance with Platonian inspiration, God is good for Boethius. Everything imperfect exists in dependence on the perfect. The perfect has an inevitable ontological priority and it is not possible to think of the imperfect without the assumption of the perfect. The perfect exists in a more real way than the imperfect. Boethius therefore anticipates later proofs of existence of God from the degrees of perfectness inspired by Platonian thought that the imperfect assumes the idea of the perfect.

Boethius is the first medieval representative of the so-called problem of universals. He tends to agree with Aristotelians claiming that generalities (universals) really exist. These are only thought entities which are based on truly existing entities or actual particularities. Interestingly, he points out that the general forms (species) are not just abstracted from particularities but they allow our thinking spirit to remember the a priori forms and universal essences. It is the evocation of latently existing, it is remembering. To some extent, Boethius' perception is ambivalent because, according to him, the universal essence always means more than just a result of thought abstraction.

The problem of freedom and inevitability (fate) is resolved by Boethius by the distinction between two levels or orders (*ordo*). He distinguishes between causal fate, i.e. the order of inevitability where there is no space for freedom and into which stoics for example also subsumed the human world, and the order of rational beings as a self-directing order of freedom. According to him, the world of intellect is the world of eternal forms as ideal forms. Therefore the more spirit there is the more freedom there is. Freedom is a function of judging intellect. The relation of intellect to the universal horizon distinguishes the plurality of possibilities. Thus, Boethius proposes an intellectualistic explanation of human freedom.

What is the relation between God, human to history and time according to Boethius? For humans, time is spread out whereas for God it is a moment. Finite and determinate beings cannot conceive events by a single immediate full act of knowledge. Divine "now" and human "now" have to be fundamentally different. However, human "now" is a dull image of the divine timeless "now". What man plans exists as present in the divine intuitive simultaneous knowledge. He inevitably gets to know free action in its facticity.

3. Pseudo-Dionysius the Areopagite

The work of Boethius implicitly points to a fundamental inner danger which was inherent to the nature of scholastic philosophy and theology from its inception. It was excessive rationalism, But in what sense? Boethius insisted on an inevitable mutual bond of belief and intellect. The "revelation" would surely be inaccessible to man if it was not somehow compatible and congruous with his intellect, if it was not rationally perceivable. This conviction can be understood as a principle. Faith without some basal understanding would not even be possible. Hermeneutical understanding is necessary even for faith. Scholastics is characterised by a great faith in the cognitive skills of man from its beginning.

How to perceive the rational understanding of faith? If we insisted on an exclusive rational understanding the mystery would be excluded and thus faith itself as well. In this sense, it is possible to talk about the danger of excessive rationalism in scholastics, rationalism which would not accept the existence of anything super-rational, anything that exceeds rationality. Therefore, scholastics involves a danger of overestimating the rational andthe scope of argumentative deductive thinking, which we can demonstrate via Boethius' rational reflections on the mystery of Trinity. In the work of Thomas Aquinas, this becomes obvious from his use of the term *demonstratio* which is commonly translated as evidence however in the context of scholastics it instead meant as simple and common reasoning. Despite this tendency, medieval scholars manage to avoid this ever present danger. Pseudo-Dionysius the Areopagite is a personification of the reason which hindered this danger.

He is a mysterious person hidden behind a pseudonym which refers to the speech of Paul the Apostle from Tarsus about an unknown god in Areopag about whom the Acts talk. We do not know who it was, despite the fact that there are 4 Greek scripts and 10 letters preserved under his name. Namely, it is the scripts *Peri Mystikes Theologias* (On Mystical Theology), *Peri Theion Onomaton* (On the Divine *Names*), *Peri tes Ekklestiastikes Hierarchias* (On the Ecclesiastical Hierarchy) and *Peri tes Uranias Hierarchias* (On the Celestial Hierarchy).

The author himself claims that he is a student of Paul the Apostle and a witness of the death of Jesus' mother.

However according to historians, he is actually a Syrian contemporary of Boethius. His scripts point at the year 500. However, why would the real author disguise his identity? There are several possible explanations: Perhaps a Neoplatonian novice tried to enhance the authority of his messages by ascribing the authorship to an Athenian. Or maybe he was trying to add more credibility to a dubitable text. The doubts concerning the authorship occurred when the texts first appeared. Despite the fact that Bishop Hypatius of Ephesus doubted these texts in 532, Pope Gregory the Great accepted them without any hesitation in the 7th century, and Maximus the Confessor wrote a commentary on them. From the 7th century onwards, the corpus of these texts was increasingly recognised and understood as an "almost Bible". The texts of Pseudo-Dionysius certainly had more influence on the Middle Ages than the work of Augustine. After their translation into Latin by Johannes Scotus Eriugena, their influence became even greater. At the peak of the Middle Ages, these texts were commented on by Albertus Magnus and Thomas Aquinas, who quoted them in their works more than 1700 times.

The identity of the author is obscured once again in the 9th century. In 827, the French king Louis the Pious received all four of Areopagite's scripts from the Byzantine emperor Michael. After that, Louis the Pious asked Abbot Hilduin from Saint-Denis to collect information about Dionysius the Parisian bishop and martyr from the 3rd century. Abbot Hilduin consequently writes *Vita Dionysii*. Furthermore, in the 13th century one can also find an opinion that the author was one of the greatest masters of the university in Paris. Therefore, there is a triple obscuration of the identity of the author: a student of Paul the Apostle, a martyr and bishop and university master. Despite these difficulties in uncovering the identity of the author, it was thanks to him that certain elements remained present in the Latin West during the entire Middle Ages, elements which would have probably otherwise been repressed by excessive rationality. This corrective moment can be understood as concern, correction or reason by mystery.

Pseudo-Dionysius understands God as a cause and essence of the life of everything; as the one who calls everything into existence, as One, as Perfect, as *hyperusia*. According to him, in God, there are ideas as models of things (*paradeigmata*). From God the world arises by emanation, but not in a pantheistic way, but on the basis of the perspective of *grades of being* and an idea of *participation*.

More concrete influences of the work of Pseudo-Dionysius Areopagite on scholastics can be described in three ways. (1) Thanks to him, the initial western orientation on *ordo* (order) gained greater breadth and power. By directing attention towards the dynamic hierarchy of grades of being and all beings, he shifted the thinking from a static perspective to a dynamic one. (2) Pseudo-Dionysius further elaborated the idea of grades of perfection which then never receded and was adopted by all mystics of the Middle Ages. The way to God, the way of knowledge and experience comprises three phases. It leads one through purification (*catharsis*), to enlightenment (*photimos*) and finally to unification with God (*teleiosis*), to rational intuition of God. (3) His third and probably his most influential idea became the *idea of negative philosophy and theology,* which is developed mostly in the works "On the Divine *Names" and "*On Mystical Theology". Here, the author poses a question about the adequate name of God. Not even a "revealed" name can be adequate for God. It is because the divine being cannot be articulated by a finite intellect. Our notions like "justice" or "good" come from a contingent empiric experience. In the case of God, justice and good are of a different genre than the ones we would like to ascribe to him on the basis of our experience. It is not possible to adequately ascribe any name to God. Moreover it is not even possible to claim that God exists or is real because he exists in a way which is not derivable from the existence of things in the world. Therefore, it is only possible to say who or what God is not, rather than who or what he is. Not even these negations are the definite knowledge of God. Pseudo-Dionysius finishes with a rational negation of the negation itself. It is because God exceeds any statement whether it is positive or negative. It is a rational argumentation about God who infinitely exceeds the possibilities of human knowledge.

What does the author himself say about it? "That while it possesses all the positive attributes of the universe (being the universal Cause), yet in a stricter sense It does not possess them, since It transcends them all, wherefore there is no contradiction between affirming and denying that It has them inasmuch as It precedes and surpasses all deprivation, being beyond all positive and negative distinctions?" (*O mystickej teológii*, I, 2). "Unto this Darkness which is beyond Light we pray that we may come, and may attain unto vision through the loss of sight and knowledge, and that in ceasing thus to see or to know we may learn to know that which is beyond all perception and understanding (for this emptying of our faculties is true sight and knowledge), 524 and that we may offer Him that transcends all things the praises of a transcendent hymnody, which we shall do by denying or removing all things that are—like as men who, carving a statue out of marble, remove all the impediments that hinder the clear perceptive of the latent image and by this mere removal display the hidden statue itself in its hidden beauty. Now we must wholly distinguish this negative method from that of positive statements. For when we were making positive statements we began with the most universal statements, and then through intermediate terms we came at last to particular titles, but now ascending upwards from particular to universal conceptions we strip off all qualities in order that we may attain a naked knowledge of that Unknowing which in all existent things is enwrapped by all objects of knowledge, and that we may begin to see that super-essential Darkness which is hidden by all the light that is in existent things." (Ibid., II).

"Once more, ascending yet higher we maintain that It is not soul, or mind, or endowed with the faculty of imagination, conjecture, reason, or understanding; nor is It any act of reason or understanding; nor can It be described by the reason or perceived by the understanding, since It is not number, or order, or greatness, or littleness, or equality, or inequality, and since It is not immovable nor in motion, or at rest, and has no power, and is not power or light, and does not live, and is not life; nor is It personal essence, or eternity, or time; nor can It be grasped by the understanding since It is not knowledge or truth; nor is It kingship or wisdom; nor is It one, nor is It unity, nor is It Godhead or Goodness; nor is It a Spirit, as we understand the term, since It is not Sonship or Fatherhood; nor is It any other thing such as we or any other being can have knowledge of; nor does It belong to the category of non-existence or to that of existence; nor do existent beings know It as it actually is, nor does It know them as they actually are; nor can the reason attain to It to name It or to know It; nor is it darkness, nor is It light, or error, or truth; nor can any affirmation or negation apply to it; for while applying affirmations or negations to those orders of being that come next to It, we apply not unto It either affirmation or negation, inasmuch as It transcends all affirmation by being the perfect and unique Cause of all things, and transcends all negation by the pre-eminence of Its simple and absolute nature-free from every limitation and beyond them all." (Ibid., V).

The fundamental corrective influence of *Corpus Dionysiacum* on medieval thinking can be demonstrated in a more concrete way. Let us take the example of of the work of Thomas Aquinas, who incorporated this non-scholastic element of negative philosophy and theology into his thinking, as an opposite of ratio and the influence of this element on his work became stronger over time. Already in the introduction to his *Summa Theologiae*, he says: "Because we do not know about God who he is but only who he is not, we cannot even think how he is but rather how he is not!" He refers to Pseudo-Dyonysius every time he talks about the so-called inaccessible darkness of the basis of all reality, about the darkness that surrounds the domain lit by arguing reason. In *Questiones Distutatae*, he claims: "The ultimate human knowledge about God is this: knowing that we do not know God."

To conclude, we can say that it is not only a question of philosophical theology but also of self-evaluation of intellect as such. The intellectual richness of this tradition can be found also at the end of the Middle Ages in the work of Nicholas of Cusa and his *teaching on known unknowingness*. The belief that everything real is eventually inscrutable is a mystery. In German mysticism, this intellectual goldmine can be seen in the work of Meister Eckhart, Edith Stein and authors associated with the putative theological turn in phenomenology of 20th century (Jean-Luc Marion, Michel Henry, and others).

4. Carolingian Renaissance

The Carolingian Renaissance conditionally related to the development of the school system. It was the developing school system that created its structural basis and made it possible. What did the transition from the ancient period and the school of antiquity to a Carolingian school look like in short? Can we say that the antique school ceased to exist in Europe at the time of the conquest of the Western Roman Empire? First of all, we have to distinguish between northern parts of the Empire, where the school system was destroyed and disappeared, and the Mediterranean parts of the continent in which Goths and Vandals represented just a minority among other institutions, but preserved schools as well.

In 533, Senator Cassiodorus wrote to the senate in the name of Ostrogoth king Athalaric: "And therefore, in order to show that sciences deserve reward, we decided that it is godless to deprive the teachers of youth of anything ... Therefore, we want every professor of sciences along with the grammarians, rhetors and teachers of law to receive the same salary as their predecessor without any decrease ... Because when we pay actors for the entertainment of people then, for much more serious reasons, we have to support those who take care of the morals and who cultivate command of words in our palace" (Cassiodorus: *Variae*, IX, 21). The same thing was implemented by the Byzantine Emperor Justinian who kept the same salaries of teachers after re-conquering Italy in 554. However in Gallia and in Spain, the schools ceased to exist in 480. However the tradition of classical education was preserved in noble families. The first teacher there was a major-domo. Their curriculum, however, was limited mostly to grammar and rhetoric and dialectics was overlooked despite Boethius' significant work. In Britain, some sort of a tutor model was preserved. It was an adapted type of druidical model of education. For example, Abbess Hilda of Whitby (614 – 680) used to receive members of aristocracy in her monastery in order for them to receive education.

During the reign of Pope Gregory the Great (540 – 604) an increase in the number of schools educating clerics and monks can be observed. Similarly there were more parish and pontifical schools. However, it is a period full of doubts about the value of classical education. For example, at the council in Vaison, the bishop

Caesarius of Arles (+542) ordered the education of small children by priests and established a boarding school in his pontifical residence.

Monasteries and abbeys were increasingly becoming the centres of education during the 7th and 8th centuries. It was in these institutions where the *Ethymologies* of Isidore of Seville and Cassiodorus' *Institutiones* and *De Orthographia* were created. It was Cassiodorus who established the big classical library in southern Italy in Vivarium. However there were not just Christian scripts in its collection and it is a testimony to the triumph over the initial close-minded monacal culture by a broader cultural vision. Cassiodorus explicitly asked monks not to forget the wealth of *humanae litterae* which was threatened by destruction of educational institutions.

The development of the school network was an institutional predisposition of the Carolingian Renaissance along with an unprecedented cultural boom of the west Frankish Empire which is related to the name of Charlemagne (742 – 814), who was crowned Emperor of the Romans by the Pope in 800 in Rome. This translation and re-connection with antique heritage was symbolised by the incorporation of segments of the church in Ravenna (6th century) into Charlemagne's chapel in Aachen. Even in this material way, the *translatio studii* and *imperii* were expressed.

However, the Carolingian Renaissance is mostly related to Charlemagne's assistant monk Alcuin of York (730 – 804). Charlemagne got to know of him in 781 in Parma and made him responsible for his court school and his personal adviser in the area of education and clerical politics. Thus, in his fifties, Alcuin left Britain. In Charlemagne's name, he was writing letters and preparing basic documents. In one of his letters to the emperor, he wrote that he wanted to be a witness of the establishment of a new Athens in France.

Alcuin's literary corpus is very large, innovative and it includes texts from diverse scientific disciplines and spheres. Alcuin was convinced that the study of the Bible (scripturistics) must be based on a serious knowledge of the seven liberal arts and that philosophy as a profane wisdom needs to support the spiritual wisdom (*sapientia spiritualis*) that it was its pre-stage. He revised the teaching of grammar and he included logic into the curriculum again. His tractate *De dialectica* became an elementary introduction to logic and it was the first work of this kind after Boethius.

Alcuin understood philosophy as a form of dialectics. In his partly philosophical script *De fide Sanctae et individuae Trinitas*, he elaborated the teaching of categories: According to him, categories were created by ten types of human statements and they do not refer to grammatical relations, but to reality. In the case of universals (see below), Alcuin advocated an extreme realistic position.

Another important author of this kind was Rabanus Maurus (784 – 856) who was Alcuin's student, and an abbot in Fulda called *praeceptor Germaniae* by the Germans. He was a theologian and polyhistor, encyclopaedist in the tradition of Cassiodorus, Isidorus of Seville, Alan ab Insulis, William of Conches, Thierry of Chartres or Vincent of Beauvais. *De Rerum Naturis* (On nature) consists of 22 books of natural encyclopaedias and is considered to be his most important work. His script of hymns *De Praedestinantione* (On Predestination) are still part of Christian liturgy (*Veni sancte Spiritus, Veni creator Spiritus*) and could be mentioned as well.

5. Johannes Scotus Eriugena

Johannes Scotus Eriugena (810 – 877) is considered to be the most philosophically relevant author of this period. From the year 840 until his death, he lived at the court of Charles the Bald where he taught liberal arts.

Eriugena contributed to the tradition of teaching seven liberal arts by introducing the script *Satira de nuptiis Philologiae et Mercurii* by the pagan author Martianus Capella (5th century) into schools, and by commenting on it in his work *Annontiationes in Martianum*. By doing this, he significantly contributed to knowledge of nature as the space of divine revelation. However, his influence on the tradition of the teaching of the liberal arts was much broader. Within these arts he supported the development of individual philosophical disciplines. In dialectics he contributed to development of logic, noetics and metaphysics. In grammar he aided development of the basics of philosophy of language. He was also influential thanks to his translations of Pseudo-Dionysius Areopagite, Gregory of Nyssa and Maximus the Confessor.

We also have to mention his involvement in the dispute about the freedom of human will, which took place in the context of a confrontation with the Benedictine monk, theologian and poet Gottschalk (805 – 868). Gottschalk's teaching on predestination and three sorts of divinity, creation of man and Eucharist was provoking passionate polemics among scholars and authors across the continent. He was opposed by many, including but not limited to the theologian Paschasius Radbertus (785 – 865), Ratramnus of Corbie, Lupus Servatus and Florus of Lyons. Fully in the tradition of anti-pelagian accentuation of divine mercy, Gottschalk underestimated the importance of human deeds for salvation. He advocated an existence of two sorts of predestination according to which the deeds of people are unimportant. It was a variant of a medieval opinion that baptism automatically guarantees salvation. However it should not be understood as a specific theological argument because this opinion was threatening social order: if the quality of human deeds was irrelevant, society would be under threat of moral erosion. Gottschalk's opinions were condemned in two synods also thanks to Eriugena's argumentation.

Eriugena devoted himself to polemics with Gottschalk in a script *De Divina Predestinatione*. The basis of his argumentation was the analysis of the notion of "God".

According to him, logic is the mother of sciences and a consistent text should consist of chaining syllogisms. Therefore, the notion of predestination depends on the notion of God, which is characterised by unity and indivisibility. Two sorts of predestination would however be in contradiction with the notion of God. At the same time, what there is not, what is nothing, God does not know and does not predestine, He only knows how it will happen. And evil is such. Consequently, human deeds matter and bad deeds simply weaken the natural connection with good. In this context, historians rightfully acknowledge Eriugena's humanising mission of the Middle Ages.

What is the relation between intellect and faith according to Eriugena? In his work, it becomes obvious that the philosophy with which he identifies seven liberal arts is gradually becomes a discipline independent from theology. Eriugena understands knowledge as a process, and liberal arts and theology as its necessary part. It is an innovated Augustinian concept: the real philosophy has to correspond to real theology. They are parts of a single cognitive process which points at *visio beatifica Dei*. Knowledge cannot happen outside faith but within it. The role of intellect is to enable apprehensibility of supernatural and hidden meaning and therefore intellect becomes the medium of truth. In this sense, the bold Eriugena's statement can be understood: "Nobody will go to heaven other than through philosophy."

It can be demonstrated in a specific image of connection between philosophy and theology: in a traditional concept of two spheres of the cosmos. The lower sphere consists of changing components (earth, water, air, fire) and the higher sphere from stable ether. Eriugena does not stress detachedness but mutual dynamic pervasion of both spheres.

Eriugena's most important work is his script *Peri Fyseon*, or *De Divisione Naturae* in Latin. It is an ambitious project of a description of the whole existence which adumbrates summas of the high Middle Ages. In this work, Eriugena tries to examine the structure and composition of the world as a whole through two notions: "division" and "nature". He reaches the conclusion that all existence can be divided into four types by four distinction. That is, into four types of nature: (1) the first is nature which creates and is not created (God, principle without principle). (2) The second is nature which is created and creates. This includes the archetypal world of primary causes, nature and causes subsisting in Word without co-essentiality with God. (3) The third consists of nature which is created and does not create, i.e. created and non-creating nature, categories of indivisible space-time that precede all created things and potential existence. (4) The fourth is nature which is neither created nor creates, God is the aim of all things, their return and rest. The assumption of this division is the fact that the lower grade of nature is a denial of the attributes of the higher grade, the lower is in non-existence compared to the higher. We can also apply this to grades of intelligibility since the higher grades are not intelligible for the lower ones.

Let us read directly from Eriugena's text: "Teacher: The division of nature seems to me to admit four species through four differentiae. The first is the division into what creates and is not created; the second into what is created and creates; the third, into what is created and does not create; the fourth, into what neither creates nor is created. Of these four, two pairs consist of opposites. The third is the opposite of the first, the fourth of the second. But the fourth is among the things which are impossible, and its differentiae are its inability to be. Does such a division seem to you correct or not?

Student: It surely does, but would you please go over it to clarify the opposition of the species just mentioned?

Teacher: Unless I'm mistaken, you see the opposition of the third species to the first. The first creates and is not created, and its opposite is that which is created and does not create. Likewise the opposition of the second to the fourth, since the second is created and creates; the fourth, which neither creates nor is created, is contrary to it in every respect.

Student: I see that clearly, but I am quite perplexed about the fourth species which you added. As for the other three, I should not venture to have any misgivings; for I judge that the first is understood in the Cause of all things which have and all which do not have being, the second in the primordial causes, the third in those things known by generation in time and place. I see, therefore, that we must have a more detailed discussion about the individual species.

Teacher: You are quite right. But I leave it to your judgment to determine our order of reasoning; i.e., to decide which species of nature should be discussed first.

Student: I think that it would be proper, before dealing with the others to say what our insight reveals to us about the first.

Teacher: All right, but I think that first we must talk briefly about the highest and main division of all which, as we said, is the division into the things which have and those which do not have being.

Student: That is a very sound and judicious idea. I see that our reasoning should begin no other way, not only because that is the first differentia of all things, but also because it appears, and is, more obscure than the others.

Teacher: Well, then, the original distinguishing differentia of all things demands clear-cut methods of interpretation. Of these, the first seems to be the one by which reason persuades us that all things subject to corporeal sense or the perception of intelligence can reasonably be said to have being; but all that, by the excellence of their nature, elude not only the hylion, i.e., every sense, but also intellect and reason, properly seem not to have being. They are correctly understood only in God, matter, and the reasons and essences of all things created by Him. And that is as it should be; for He Himself, who alone truly has being, is the essence of all things, according to Dionysius the Areopagite, who says: "The being of all things is Superbeing, Divinity." Gregory the Theologian too affirms by many reasons that intellect or reason cannot grasp what any substance or essence is, whether it belongs to visible or to invisible creation. For just as God Himself, in Himself, beyond all creation is grasped by no intellect, so also ousia ["essentia" or "being"] considered in the inner most recesses of the creation made by Him and existing in Him, is incomprehensible. Besides, whatever in every creature is either perceived by corporeal sense or considered by the intellect is simply some accident, incomprehensible in itself, as has been said, of an essence (accidens essentiae). By quality, quantity, form, matter, some differentia, place, or time we know not what it is (quid est), but that it is (quia est). This, then, is the first and highest method of division of what is said to have and what is said not to have being. I believe, however, that that method, which it seems, in a way, possible to introduce, namely the one based on privations of states in reference to substances, as sight and blindness in reference to the eyes, must be utterly rejected. For if something wholly lacks being and cannot be and does not surpass intellect because of the supernal height of its existence, I fail to see how it can fit into the divisions of things;

unless, perhaps, one should say that the absences and privations (absentia et privatio) of things with being are not absolutely nothing (non omnino nihil esse), but that they are contained by some remarkable natural power of those things of which they are the privations, absences, or opposites, so that, in a certain way, they have being (ut quoddam modo sint).

Let us grant that the second method of being and not-being is the one considered in the orders and differentiae (ordinibus atque differentiis consideratur) of created natures. Beginning from the most exalted intellectual power stationed closest to God, it descends to the extreme of rational and irrational creation. To speak more clearly, I mean from the highest angel to the lowest part of a rational or irrational soul, the vital principle of nutrition and growth (for when the soul is considered as a genus, the part of the soul which nurtures the body and causes it to grow is the lowest). Here each order, including the bottommost order of bodies with which all division is terminated, can be said in a remarkable way to have and not to have being. What is stated affirmatively of the lower is stated negatively of the higher. Likewise what is stated negatively of the lower is stated affirmatively of the higher. In the same way, what is stated affirmatively of the higher is stated negatively of the lower; and what is stated negatively of the higher will be stated affirmatively of the lower. What is stated affirmatively of a man, that he is still mortal, is stated negatively of an angel. What is stated negatively of a man is stated affirmatively of an angel, and vice versa. For example, if a man is a rational, mortal, visible animal (animal rationale, mortale, risibile), an angel is surely not a rational, mortal, visible animal. Similarly, if an angel is an essential motion of the intellect focusing on God and the causes of things, surely man is not an essential motion of the intellect focusing on God and the causes of things. The same rule can be observed in all celestial essences until one reaches the highest order of all which is terminated above by the Supreme Negation. Its negative definition affirms that no creature is higher than It. There are three orders called homotageis ("of equal rank"). The first of these consists of Cherubim, Seraphim, and Thrones; the second of Virtues, Powers, and Dominations; the third of Principalities, Archangels, and Angels. In descending order, the lowest group of bodies merely negates or affirms what is higher than itself because it has nothing beneath itself to take away or add since it is preceded by all higher orders and does not precede anything lower than itself. Similarly for this reason, every order of rational and intellectual creature is said to have and not to have being. It has being insofar as it is known by higher creatures or by itself; it lacks being insofar as it does not allow itself to be comprehended by its inferiors.

The third method is fittingly observed in the things with which the fullness of this visible world is made complete, and in their prior causes in the innermost recesses of nature (in secretissimis naturae sinibus). For whatever of the causes themselves is known by generation in time and place in formed matter is said, by human convention, to have being. Whatever, on the other hand, is still contained within the recesses of nature and does not appear in formed matter or in place, time, or the other accidents, is said, by the same human convention, not to have being. Clear examples of this kind abound, particularly in human nature. For God formed all men together in that single first man (primo atque uno) who He made in His own image, but He did not bring them forth at the same time into this visible world. Rather, at set times and places in a sequence known to Himself He brings into visible essence the nature which He had formed together. Thus those who now visibly appear in the world and who have appeared are said to have being. Those who still lie hidden, but are destined to be, are said not to have being. This is the difference between the first and third methods. The first is seen generally in all things made once and together in their causes and effects. The third is seen specifically in the things which partly still lie hidden in their causes and partly are revealed in their effects; and of these the fabric of this world is properly woven. To this method belongs the reason which considers the power of seeds (virtutem seminum considerat), whether in animals, trees, or grasses. The power of the seeds, while it lies still in the secret recesses of nature, is said not to have being because it does not yet appear. Once it has appeared, however, in the birth and growth of animals, flowers, or the fruits of trees and grasses, it is said to be.

The fourth method, according to the plausible theory of philosophers, states that only those things grasped by the intellect alone (solo intellectu) truly have being; that whatever things are varied, collected, or dissolved through generation, by the expansion or contraction of matter, and by local and temporal motions — e.g., all bodies, which can be born and destroyed (nasci et corrumpi) — are truly said not to have being.

The fifth method is the one which reason observes only in human nature. When through sin it abandoned the dignity of the divine image in which it had properly subsisted, it deservedly lost its being and therefore is said not to have being. When it is restored by the grace of God's only - begotten Son to the original condition of its substance in which it was created in God's image, it begins to have being and to be alive in Him who was created in God's image. It is evidently to this method that the following statement of the Apostle relates: "And He calls the things which have no being, just as those which do." [Romans 4:17] That is, God the Father calls those lost in the first man and fallen to a kind of substancelessness to have being through faith in His Son like those already reborn in Christ. This method may also be understood, however, as relating to those whom God calls daily from the hidden recesses of nature, in which they are thought not to have being, into visible appearance in form, matter, and the other things in which the hidden can appear. Perhaps a keener reason can discover something besides these methods (praeter hos modos), but I think that enough has been said about these matters for the present, unless you disagree." (*Peri fyseón*, I, 1-7).

According to Eriugena, three out of four natures relate to God directly: They are forms of his being. First, second and fourth nature manifest three forms of the same, for the created world a transcendent God, while the third nature is a specific form of divine immanence. This perspective however cannot be treated as a *theophany* of God in the natural world. God himself is the union of these ontological processes. He unifies all four natures and at the same time he creates and is being created. All good in this process of events is the good of participationin the first nature. How to understand this? Eriugena claims that God cannot be just the cause, middle and aim but also the ontological environment of the whole course of events. God is being created when he creates because he is the essence of everything that exists. It does not mean anything other than the fact that God constitutes the nature of things in which He Himself is revealed. This dynamic understanding of God is also justified etymologically by Eriugena: "Of this name [then] an etymology has been taken over from the Greeks: for either it is derived from the verb (*theoro*), that is, "I see"; or from the verb (*theo*), that is, "run"; or – which is more likely [since] the meaning of both is [one and] the same – it is correctly held to be derived from both. For when it is derived from the verb (*theoro*), (*theos*) is interpreted to mean "he who sees," for He sees in Himself all things that are [while] He looks upon nothing that is outside Himself because outside Him there is nothing. But when (*theos*) is derived from the verb (*theo*) it is correctly interpreted as "he who runs," for He runs throughout all things and never stays but His running fills out all things, as it is written: "His Word runneth swiftly." [And yet He is not moved at all. For of God] it is most truly said that He is motion at rest and rest in motion. For He is at rest unchangingly in Himself, never departing from the stability of His Nature; yet He sets Himself in motion through all things in order that those things which essentially subsist by Him may be. For by His motion all things are made. And thus there is one and the same meaning in the two interpretations of the same name, which is God. For in God to run through all things is not something other than to see all things, but as by His seeing so too by His running all things are made." (Ibid., I, 12).

In this context, Eriugena could be understood as Hegel of the 9th century. According to him, God is present in the world through a theophany. God is not just the divine essence but also the way of being by which the God manifests himself in the created world. He elevates it to himself and thus it is the highest act of the ontological process which unfolds from nature which is not created and creates, to the nature which is not created and does not create. The world and humans return to God. The events in the first and second nature happen in eternity or in timelessness, while the creation happens as a journey back to God in time and it has an ascendant (rising) character. Here, Eriguena also integrates the opinions about the creation of man trying to understand materiality as a consequence of sin. In the fourth nature, the return to immateriality occurs and man becomes a "second God" in some analogical way.

According to Eriugena, in the fullest sense, the epiphany of God happens in man as a rational being. Eriugena's argument affirming the exceptional position of man is admirable. Man is extraordinary thanks to the fact that he unifies all possible diversity in an extraordinary way. He unifies rationality with sensuality, immateriality and materiality and thus he integrates all differences in himself while he does not achieve unity which would obliterate and eliminate these differences. We can recognise a similarity to the antique conception of a small cosmos in it, where man is sort of a miniature of cosmos. However Eriugena claims, that man as an image of God cannot be just a miniature of the world, because he elevates it above himself.

Eriugena argues that man in his (third) natureanticipates the perfection of the fourth nature in cognition: Thanks to the immaterial categories of quantity and quality in his intellect, he conceives material which leads him to an idea similar to that of Nicholas of Cusa (1401 – 1464): the material exists thanks to human cognition. A certain similarity can also be found in the work of Thomas Aquinas (1225 – 1274) according to whom man, thanks to cognition perceiving the essences of things, elevates sensory objects by conceiving them in their more perfect form than the one in which they exist in material reality.

Eriugena understands knowledge as illumination and thus can be included in the medieval tradition of illuminism, which extends from Plotinus (204/5 – 270) through to Augustine to Franciscans, to Comenius (1592 – 1670) and Capuchin Valeriano Magni (1586 – 1661). Unfortunately, the complicated work of Johannes Scotus Eriugena did not always find understanding readers. After its great influence, which it enjoyed during the Carolingan Renaissance, it was later refused as an "Irish mash". In the high Middle Ages, his work was condemned in Paris in 1210 and also in the lateran council in 1215 together with scripts of Amalric of Bena (1140/1150 – 1206). In 1225 it was prohibited by Pope Honorius II himself under a threat of "death sentence". In a shallow and simplified way, it was read as pantheistic. Its renaissance took place only thanks to Nicholas of Cusa.

6. Anselm of Canterbury

The end of 8th and the whole of the 9th century was a period of extensive cultural renewal and rich literary production. Old texts were evaluated and rewritten, as were commentaries, encyclopaedias and glosses. It could be said that this period left a whole Latin literary corpus. The nature of the literature of the 10th century is already different. It is not organically related to the school system nor to the evaluation of the old anymore. Its characteristics are self-confidence and self-reflection.

Despite the fact that the 11th century is often overlooked as a transitional century between the 10th century Ottonian Renaissance and the significant 12th century, from a philosophical point of view, we have to pay attention to it and take a closer examination of some of its scholars.

An important scholar of the 11th century was Anselm of Canterbury (1033 – 1109) who is rightfully considered to be the "father of scholastics" and, after Eriugena, was the first real philosopher of the Middle Ages. Anselm was the most important student of Lanfranc in a prominent monastic school in Bec and later he became its prior. From 1093, Anselm was the archbishop of Canterbury.

Anselm formulated his understanding of the relation between faith and intellect in a statement that faith searches for understanding (*"fides quaerns intellectum"*). In an introduction to a famous script *Proslogion* (Speech to You), Anselm claims that he does not need intellect in order to believe but he believes in order to understand not only the supernatural, but also the world as a whole. Philosophy and theology are an inseparable pair from Anselm's perspective. In his work, the transition from monacal theology to scientific theology is accomplished. A great intellectual freedom intertwined with passionate interest radiates from his letter *Cur Deus Homo* (Why did God Become Human?) addressed to Pope Urban II.

According to Anselm, intellect which wants to serve faith should be engaged in its own sphere. Anselm believes that the most convincing statements for faith should be those which do not arise from faith but are the result of rational argumentation. The result of this conviction is the aforementioned work *Proslogion*, in which he attempts to base faith in indubitable recognition of the existence of God. In relation to faith, philosophy and intellect play dual role: they make faith possible; they deepen it however not in the sense of the sole and necessary precondition. Intellect, however, is also a mediator of faith and sight (*visio*). Intellect as *intellectus* bridges faith and intellectively perceiving vision.

Anselm is known to the history of philosophy mostly as a creator of arguments regarding the existence of God and especially of the *ontological argument* of existence of God. In *Monologion* (Speech to Myself), Anselm elaborates three arguments of existence of God. (1) The first refers to the empirically evident grades of good, ontological nobility (degree of perfection) and the consequential recognition of the existence of good above which no better good can be conceived. (2) The second one is devoted to a similar analysis of the "highest" and (3) the third is devoted to "perfection and simplicity". The third and final argument refers to a conviction that everything we encounter in the world is not inevitable but conditional, and that everything conditional has to be based on something inevitable, unconditioned, something which is being *per se*, for itself and not through something else, *per aliud*. Here, Anselm interprets the relation between the world and God analogically in relation to *substance* and *accident*. However, for Anselm himself, these chain arguments realised in *Proslogion* are not sufficient and he strives for an argument which would be sufficient in itself. It is an attempt to find something indubitable which would support the dubitative intellect and the conditioned human existence. Anselm proposes this kind of argument in the introduction of *Proslogion*:

"Therefore, O Lord, You who give understanding to faith, grant me to understand — to the degree You know to be advantageous — that You exist, as we believe, and that You are what we believe [You to be]. Indeed, we believe You to be something than which nothing greater can be thought. Or is there, then, no such nature [as You], for the Fool has said in his heart that God does not exist? But surely when this very same Fool hears my words "something than which nothing greater can be thought," he understands what he hears. And what he understands is in his understanding, even if he does not understand [i.e., judge] it to exist. For that a thing is in the understanding is distinct from understanding that [this] thing exists. For example, when a painter envisions what he is about to paint: he indeed has in his understanding that which he has not yet made, but he does not yet understand that it exists. But after he has painted [it]: he has in his understanding that which he has made, and he understands that it exists. So even the Fool is convinced that something than which nothing greater can be thought is at least in his understanding; for when he hears of this [being], he understands [what he hears], and whatever is understood is in the understanding. But surely that than which a greater cannot be thought cannot be only in the understanding. For if it were only in the understanding, it could be thought to exist also in reality — something which is greater [than existing only in the understanding]. Therefore, if that than which a greater cannot be thought were only in the understanding, then that than which a greater cannot be thought would be that than which a greater can be thought! But surely this [conclusion] is impossible. Hence, without doubt, something than which a greater cannot be thought exists both in the understanding and in reality.

Assuredly, this [being] exists so truly [i.e., really] that it cannot even be thought not to exist. For there can be thought to exist something which cannot be thought not to exist; and this thing is greater than that which can be thought not to exist. Therefore, if that than which a greater cannot be thought could be thought not to exist, then that than which a greater cannot be thought would not be that than which a greater cannot be thought — [a consequence] which is contradictory. Hence, something than which a greater cannot be thought exists so truly that it cannot even be thought not to exist. And You are this [being], O Lord our God. Therefore, O Lord my God, You exist so truly that You cannot even be thought not to exist. And this is rightly the case. For if any mind could think of something better than You, the creature would rise above the Creator and would sit in judgment over the Creator — something which is utterly absurd. Indeed, except for You alone, whatever else exists can be thought not to exist. Therefore, You alone exist most truly of all and thus most greatly of all; for whatever else exists does not exist as truly [as do You] and thus exists less greatly [than do You]. Since, then, it is so readily clear to a rational mind that You exist most greatly of all, why did the Fool say in his heart that God does not exist? — why [indeed] except because [he is] foolish and a fool!" (*Proslogion*, II-III). And so, in *Monologion*, Anselm finally claims that a real being is evident from the intentional existence of something above which nothing greater may be conceived.

A monk called Gaunilo came out against Anselm's argument with criticism in which he claimed that existence of being cannot be inevitably derived from its conceivability – even if it is most perfect in certain genus of beings. Most probably, Gaunilo overlooked the passages of *Proslogion* in which the author specifies the conditions of the validity of the given argument: he does not refer to the existence of the finite and chance being since this cannot imply the inevitability of its existence. Despite that, Anselm replies to Gaunilo in a smaller piece *Liber Apologeticus ad Insipientem*. Anselm not only finds the ontological argument for the existence of God but he also finds a definite support for the intellect and its activity.

Finally, it is the time to examine the problem of universals which is present throughout the entire Middle Ages. It is a problem of the nature of thought regarding universals, which stretches back to Porphyry, Cicero and Boethius and extreme positions which are strictly realism and nominalism, both of which were becoming dominant towards the end of the Middle Ages. This problem is related to three questions which Porphyry left open in his work *Isagoge*: (1) Do genus and species really exist or are they just a product of intellect? (2) If they do really exist, are they material or immaterial? And (3) do they exist independently from the entities or within the entities?

According to Boethius, universals exist both in entities and in intellect. In the entities, they exist in a material way and in unity with the entities while in intellect, they exist in an immaterial state and separately from entities. Boethius defined "universal" as something that is common to many and Porphyry described it as predicable to multiple.

The realistic positions on this problem which were defended during the Middle Ages can be divided into two groups: (1) The first group consists of *realists of material essence* for whom matter was just an accessible commonality for all particularities which would differ only in accidental forms. Odo of Tournai (1060 – 1113) and William of Champeaux (1070 – 1101) for example can be included in this group.

(2) The second group consists of realists of indifferentism who believed that universals had real existence which was based in the non-difference of diverse reali-

ties. According to this perspective, people we learn about successively do not differ from each other because they do not differ in their human nature. They are particularities according to differentness and universals according to their universal human nature. Alberich of Reims (1085 – 1141) could be included into this group.

The second group that disagreed with the realists was constituted by *extreme nominalists*. Roscelin of Compiègne (1050 – 1120), who was a teacher of Peter Abelard, became its significant representative. According to him, only particularities or individual beings exist. Neither genus nor species are real, and all universal designation is only verbal designation (*flatus vocis*).

Many other opinions which seek to avoid extremes can be placed on the spectrum between these two extreme positions.. This includes most of all Peter Abelard (1079 – 1142) whose position is commonly characterised as *sermonism* or *conceptualism*. For Abelard, this is rather a problem of logic and language than ontology. He concludes that "*est autem universale vocabulum quod de pluribus singillatim habile est ex inventione sua praedicari*" (Therefore, there is a universal term which is able to be individually ascribed to many according to convention). This process of ascribing the universal to an empirical singularity is called *appelatio* by Abelard and the ascription of the universal to a sensuously unperceivable entity is called *significatio* (e.g. if I talk about man as about species, it is *significatio*).

Moderate realism in the problem of universals is represented by Thomas Aquinas (1225 – 1274), for instance, and by most of authors of 13th century, who were convinced that a universal is included and predicated in many. It doesn't exist in things despite the fact that it is based in them, it exists only in intellect. For example Albert the Great distinguishes between three types of universals: the ideal (in God), the concrete (in entities) and the abstract (in notion).

Even modern and contemporary philosophy returns to this problem because behind it lies another still relevant problem of the relation of the universal to the singular. The question whether universal notions represent some reality or whether they are just artificial and conventionally accepted signs is asked by philosophers as well as logicians, mathematicians, psychologists and linguists until these days. Even thanks to this actual problem of the reality of universals, medieval philosophy addresses the modern one.

7. Peter Abelard

Another significant renaissance scholar of this period was undoubtedly the French scholar Peter Abelard (1079 – 1142). His personality combines subtle rationality, great impassionedness and engagement. In dialectics, he surpassed his teacher William of Champeaux, who consequently came to hate him, while he was still a student. Peter then continued his studies under the guidance of Anselm of Laon.

As he himself admits in *Historia Calamitatum* (A History of my Calamities) written in Paris around 1117, he seduced Heloise, an educated niece of his colleague. He was striving for her hand despite the fact that she insisted it was better to freely love each other than being bound by some agreement which would interfere with a philosophical life. Abelard's son Astrolabius was born in 1118. Heloise's uncle, Parisian canon Fulbert, had Abelard forcibly castrated, thinking that he abused his niece. Consequently Abelard forced Heloise to become a nun and he himself became a monk in Saint-Denis where he held the position of abbot and simultaneously took care of Heloise's convent.

Abelard faced different criticism of his work. His script *Theologia* was condemned by the synod of Soissons. Bernard of Clairvaux himself contributed to his conviction by the council of Sens in 1140 and even his appeal to Pope Innocent II did not help. Abelard's silence and refusal of defence in the council remains a mystery. Consequently he was accepted by Peter the Venerable in Cluny, where he lived serenely and dignifiedly and worked as a theologian and philosopher until his death. The inscription on his tombstone appropriately read "Gaelic Socrates".

In order to better understand Abelard's contribution to medieval philosophy, we have to look at his understanding of knowledge. Abelard's thinking takes place in a space defined by the radical nominalism of Roscellinus and the radical realism of William of Champeaux, and it critices realism in all its forms. Contrary to realists he claims that the general and the universal do not really exist and are created by intellect. He also refuses Roscellinus for whom the universal exists only in the voice or in speech (*vox*). However for Abelard, *vox* is not merely a medium of sound but also a medium of meaning. In this context, it is possible to say that speech is the domain of universals. Words relate to the singular and they name it (*appelatio*) or to something general which they signify (*significatio*). The word by which we signify something universal is called *vox universalis* (*voces universalis* = universals) by Abelard. This position, which transcended elements of both extreme positions, realism and nominalism, is called conceptualism or sermonism.

The framework of this understanding is Abelard's peculiar theory of knowledge. Despite the fact that he was largely influenced by Aristotle, he surpasses him and creates his own theory of abstraction. Similarly to Aristotle, he claims that notions are a product of abstract activity of intellect. However, by abstraction, he means something different than Aristotle. According to Aristotle, the process of abstraction takes place as rescinding, as conceiving of the general in the particular, as conceiving its nature or essence. Abstraction therefore uncovers the architecture of the world in its categorical structure of genus and species. For Abelard, the abstract activity of intellect is an ability to perceive different qualities of particularities separately. If any of the qualities are found in several entities, it becomes something general which is not related to a single thing. Intellect therefore does not conceive the essences of entities. The essence is inaccessible for intellect. Abelard does not deny the inevitable existence of the essence of entities, however he denies the ability of man to appropriately conceive it. According to Abelard, the way of understanding things by man cannot be identified with the way they exist. Essence is fully accessible only to God. Because of this, Abelard reaches a subjectivisation of knowledge. We do not know things in their nature and we can make general judgements about them based only on similarity. We know only the qualities of things which do not exist separately.

Notions do not reflect reality directly. According to Abelard, the so called general notions are always dark and to some extent also confusing. He demonstrates it on an example of a notion of a city: all individual cities are essentially different despite our expectations and thus also in terms of the dark notion of "city" as a city.

Because the term "general notion" suggests objectivity, Abelard decides to instead use the term "opinion". It should be an expression of a noetic humbleness which is based in the cognitive potency of man.

Because the generalities/universals exist as *nomina* in speech, they have to be specific concepts of intellect with relation to reality, but not in the way of direct reflection. They relate to each other through so called *figmenta* (*forma communis*) which regulate and form reality into cognitively acceptable image or layer for man. *Figmenta* mediate the relationship of real and intentional. We cannot talk about adequacy in the sense of *adaequatio rei et intellectus* (congruence/adequacy of thing and intellect).

The process of adequation is specifically transformed on the side of man in a way that it is not possible to talk about adequacy anymore. This is the content of subjectivisation of knowledge in work of Abelard.

Such an essential subjectivisation of knowledge had an epochal influence on all spheres of Abelard's thinking. Historians rightfully highlight Abelard as the one in whose work an emancipation of ethics from ontology takes place, since he understood ethics as an autonomous discipline with its own subject already before Thomas Aquinas. And of course, his ethics had to be consequently subjectivised as well.

Terms such as "sin" which naturally indicate aspiration for generality, for universal validity, could not play a role of universal referential moments in Abelard's concept. Sin and its relation to notions of good and evil lose their supposed general clarity in Abelard's work. If man does not have access to obvious generalities/universals, then he does not have access to general ethical norms either. Despite their existence, they are not accessible to him as generalities. It is not possible to subsume unique human actions under generally valid universal ethical norms, because they are not available to us. Good and evil therefore cannot be judged from the outside but only from inside of an acting person. In his script *Ethica*, Abelard deals with the notion of intention or aim, and he reaches a paradoxical claim that those who killed Christ were innocent, because they believed their act was right. Therefore, the place where morality or immorality of deeds is decided is not the external adequacy with a norm but only a space of the internal reflection: conscience. Only the intention can be moral or immoral. Subjectivisation of the ethics is accomplished here as an exclusive stress of intention. For these reasons, Abelard became a critic of the contemporary criminal law. For Abelard, Ethics became similar to the Socratic knowledge of oneself because the questioning of one's own intentions has to be a form of subjective responsibility and inner integrity. This is why the title "Gaelic Socrates" is so appropriate for Abelard.

Among his works, *Sic et non* (Yes and No) has to be mentioned. It is also dedicated to the relationship between philosophy and theology and it postulates a modern requirement for the logical analysis of the Bible and its terminological examination. This requirement logically resulted from Abelard's understanding of speech which is a peculiar sphere with its own structure different from that of reality and logic. He demands language analysis to be conducted before the logical and content analyses because understanding is determined by the different language employed. It can be technical or informal language, or the translation could be wrong. Here, we can see strong hermeneutic features. The significance of Abelard's demands on terminological clarity, logical correctness both in theology and philosophy paved the way for the *summas* of the high Middle Ages.

it is almost as if Abelard outlined the static possibilities of the Gothic arch, abandoning the clumsiness of the Romanesque style and made the construction of the most beautiful Gothic cathedrals possible.

Let us allow Abelard to speak for himself: "Indeed, each man is as well-stocked with words as he is with sense. And since according to Cicero (De Invent. I, 41, 76), 'A sameness in all things is the mother of weariness' (that is, it gives rise to distaste), it is fitting to vary these words used on the same topic and not to strip everything bare with casual and common words. Such topics, as blessed Augustine said, are veiled for this reason, lest they become cheap, and the greater the effort it takes to discover them and the more difficult it is to master them, the more precious they are. Likewise, it is often appropriate to change the wording to suit the differences among those with whom we speak, since it frequently happens that the proper meaning of a word is unknown or less familiar to some people. Certainly if we wish, as is fitting, to speak to these people, to teach them, we should strive after their usage, rather than after proper speech, as that leader in the grammatical arts and instructor of speaking, Priscian himself, taught. [...]

Who does not see how rash it is for one person to make a judgment concerning the sense and intelligence of another when our hearts and thoughts are revealed to God alone? He calls us back from this presumption when He says: 'Do not judge and you shall not be judged' (Luke 6:37). And the Apostle: 'Therefore pass no judgement,' he says, 'before the time, until the Lord comes, who will both bring to light the things hidden in darkness and make manifest the counsels of hearts' (1 Corinthians 4:5), as if he says openly: Entrust the judgement in such matters to Him Who alone knows all things and discerns our very thoughts. Accordingly it is also written metaphorically about the paschal lamb in reference His secret mysteries (Exodus 12:10), 'If there be anything left, you shall burn it with fire'-- that is, if there is anything remaining of the divine mysteries that we are not able to understand, let us keep what is to be taught aside for the Spirit through whom these things were written, rather than explaining them rashly.

We also ought to pay close attention so that, when some of the writings of the saints are presented to us as if they were contradictory or other than the truth, we are not misled by false attributions of authorship or corruptions in the text itself. For many apocryphal works are inscribed with the names of saints in order that they might obtain authority, and even some places in the text of the Holy Testament itself have been corrupted by scribal error. [...]

Nor is it any less a matter for consideration whether such statements are ones taken from the writings of the saints that either were retracted elsewhere by these same saints and corrected when the truth was afterwards recognised – as St. Augustine often did – or whether they spoke reflecting the opinion of others rather than according to their own judgment, just as Ecclesiastes often brings in conflicting ideas from different people, whence 'Ecclesiastes' is translated as 'provoker', (as St. Gregory asserts in his fourth Dialogue, or whether they left such statements under investigation as they were examining them rather than concluding with a confident solution, just as the aforementioned venerable doctor, Augustine, says that he did in his work On the Text of Genesis when he recalls this work in the first of his Retractions (II, xxiv, I): 'In this work,' he says, 'more things were sought after than found, and of those found, very few were confirmed –- the rest, in fact, were so proposed as still to be in need of investigation.' [...]

Poetic and philosophic writings also say many things based on opinion, as if they were steadfast in truth, things which however, are clearly quite inconsistent with the truth. Thus this passage of Ovid (Ars Amatoria I, 349-350): 'The grain is always greener in foreign fields, and the flocks of our neighbour have richer yields.'

Boethius also, when in the third book of the Topics he said accident and substance were the two primary kinds of things, was looking more to opinion than to truth. Cicero openly acknowledges that philosophers also expressed many ideas according to the opinions of others rather than their own judgement, with these words (De Officiis, II, 9-10): 'Justice has sufficient authority without wisdom, but wisdom without justice does not have the force to instil faith. For the craftier and shrewder someone is, the more envied and mistrusted he becomes when his reputation for honesty has been lost. For this reason, justice accompanied by understanding will have as much strength as it wishes to instil confidence. Justice without wisdom is capable of much, but wisdom without justice can accomplish nothing. But let no one marvel why I say this, as if it were possible for anyone to be just who is not at the same time wise; since all philosophers agree, and I myself have often argued, that whoever has one virtue has them all. The reason for this is that our type of speech is one thing when truth itself is polished in argumentation and another thing when it is entirely adapted to everyone. And therefore we are speaking here in the popular sense, when we refer to one man as brave and another as good and still others as wise. We must use common words and usage when we speak.' Finally, the usage of everyday speech is such that most things are expressed in accordance with the judgement of the bodily senses, even if the reality is otherwise. For although there is no place in the entire universe that is entirely empty and not filled either with air or some other body, still we say that a box in which we perceive nothing by sight is entirely empty. For judging according to what we see with our eyes, we say that the sky is sometimes starry, sometimes not, the sun sometimes hot and sometimes not, or that the moon gives more light or gives less, or even does not give light at all, when, however, these things which do not always appear to us uniformly, in fact always remain uniform. What is so amazing, then, if some things are proposed or even written by the Holy Fathers sometimes based on opinion rather than on the truth? When conflicting things are said about the same topic, one must carefully distinguish that which is offered with the stricture of a command, that which is offered with the lenience of indulgence and that which is offered with exhortation to perfection, so that we might seek a remedy for the apparent conflict in accordance with this variety of intents. If indeed it is a command, we must distinguish whether it is general or specific, that is, directed toward everyone in general or toward certain people in particular. [...]

No one is rationally judged to be lying when they say something false that they believe is true, because, inasmuch as one believes it, one does not deceive but is oneself deceived. Likewise, someone who holds false opinions, carelessly accepted in place of true ones, ought to be accused not of lying but of sometime rashness. On the other hand, anyone lies who says a true thing, while believing that it is false. For insofar as his intent is concerned, because he does not say what he believes, to that extent he does not speak the truth, even if what he says may actually turn out to be true. Nor is someone free from lying, if they unwittingly speak the truth, but lie insofar as their knowledge and intent. And this (*Enchiridion* 22): 'Everyone who lies speaks in contradiction to what he believes in his mind, with the intention of deceiving.' And also, in Book Two of his commentary on the Gospels (*Contra Mendacium* x, 24): 'That Jacob managed at his mother's bidding to seem to deceive his father; if examined carefully, is not a lie but rather a mystery. For a truthful [i.e. allegorical] meaning can in no way rightly be called a lie.' Indeed in this passage the spiritual teacher only accepts as a lie a transgression which God, who is the judge of hearts and passions, weighs according to the intent of the speaker rather than according to the quality of the speech, paying attention not so much to what is done as to the spirit in which it is done. According to this, anyone is guiltless insofar as they think sincerely and without falseness and do not speak deceitfully – just as it is written (Proverbs 10:9), 'He that walketh sincerely, walketh confidently.' Otherwise even the Apostle Paul might be accused of lying when he follows his own judgement rather than the truth of the matter as he writes to the Romans saying 'Therefore when I have completed this, and have delivered to them the proceeds, I will set out by way of you for Spain.' (*Romans* 15:28). Thus it is one thing to lie and another to be mistaken while speaking and to stray from the truth in one's words due to error, not to malice.

If God on occasion does allow this to happen even to the holy ones themselves, as we have said, in those situations that would cause no damage to the faith, it does not happen unproductively to those by whom everything is undertaken for the good. Even the ecclesiastical teachers themselves, diligently attentive and believing some things in their works needed correction, grant to posterity the license to emend or not to follow them; if somehow these teachers were not able to retract or correct in their works. Whence even the teacher Augustine, cited above, in Book One of his *Retractions* (prologus 2): 'It is written,' he says, 'you do not avoid sin by loquacity.' And also the apostle James says 'Let every man be swift to hear but slow to speak.' And 'For in many things we all offend. If anyone does not offend in word, he is a perfect man.' (James 1:19 and James 3:2 respectively). I do not claim this perfection for myself even now, when I am an old man – how much less when as a young man I began to write. And in the prologue to Book Three of the On the Trinity (proem 2): 'Do not defer to my writings as if they were canonical scriptures, but whatever you would find in the canonical scriptures that you did not believe, believe steadfastly. But in my writings I do not want you to accept with assurance something that you had not been taking as certain unless you now understand it as certain.' And in the letters to Vincentus Victor, Book Two (*De Anime et eius Origine* IV, 1): 'I cannot, nor should I, deny that just as I might be blamed for many things in my conduct by fair judgement without rashness, so I might be blamed for many things in my writings.' And again in his letter to Vincent (Epist. 95, x, 35), 'Do not desire, brother, to collect calumnies against such clear divine witnesses – either from our writings, or from Hilary, or from Cyprian and Agrippinus, because this type of writing should be distinguished from the authority of the canon. For they are not to be read as if it were not permissible to disagree with the testimony presented in them, if in some place they should claim to know otherwise than the truth demands.' And again to Fortunatianus (*Epist.* 148, iv, 15): 'Nor ought we to regard the arguments of anyone, no matter how Catholic and well-regarded, in the way we regard the canonical scriptures, that is (with all due respect to these men) as if we were not permitted to refute or reject something that we find in their writings where their opinions differ from the established truth. I wish my readers to hold the same attitude toward my writings as I hold toward the writings of others.' And again in the Response to Faustus (*Contra Faustum*, Book 1, Chapter xi): 'We are far from saying that Paul sometimes erred and changed his opinion as he advanced. For one could say that the books we have written, not with the authority of commanding but in the exercise of utility, are not comparable to the [canonical] books.' And again (*Contra Faustum*, XI, v): 'For we are the ones of whom the Apostle said: 'and in any point you are minded otherwise, this also God will reveal to you' – this type of writing of letters should be read not with a compulsion to believe but with the freedom to evaluate. However, so that the room for this freedom is not excluded, and that very healthy task of treating difficult questions and translating their language and style is not denied to later authors, the excellence of the canonical authority of the Old and New Testaments has been distinguished from that of the works of later authors. [...]

With these prefatory words, it seems right, as we have undertaken to collect the diverse sayings of the Holy Fathers, which stand out in our memory to some extent due to their apparent disagreement as they focus on an issue; this may lure the weaker readers to the greatest exercise of seeking the truth, and may render them sharper readers because of the investigation. Indeed this first key of wisdom is defined, of course, as assiduous or frequent questioning. Aristotle, the most clear-sighted philosopher of all, advised his students, in his preface 'Ad Aliquid', to embrace this questioning with complete willingness, saying (cited by Boethius, In *Categorias Aristotelis*, II): 'Perhaps it is difficult to clarify things of this type with confidence unless they are dealt with often and in detail. However, it would not be useless to have some doubts concerning individual points.' And indeed, through doubting we come to questioning and through questions we perceive the truth. In consequence of this, Truth herself says (Matthew 7:7), 'Ask and it shall be given you; knock and it shall be opened to you.' Teaching us this spiritual lesson with Himself as an example, He let Himself be found, at about twelve years of age, sitting and questioning in the midst of the teachers, showing Himself to us in the model of a student with His questioning, before that of a schoolmaster in his pronouncements, although His knowledge of God was full and complete. And when some passages of Scripture are brought before us, the more the authority of the Scripture itself is commended, the more fully they excite the reader and tempt him to seek the truth. Hence it seemed good to me to prefix to my work here (this work of mine which we have compiled out of passages from holy authors, gathered into one volume), the decree of Pope Gelasius concerning authentic books, so that it can be understood that we have included no passages from apocryphal writings here. We also append excerpts from the Retractions of blessed Augustine, from which it may be clear that nothing set forth here is taken from passages that he later emended when he made his retraction." (*Prologue to Sic et Non*).

Doubtfulness and doubting become Abelard's principles as it can be seen in the text above. His analysis includes semantics, textual and literary critique; it counts on education and it concludes that the "Real key leading to wisdom is restless and frequent doubt ... Because we arrive to examination through doubt, we perceive truth through examination; therefore the Truth itself said: 'Search and you will find.'" Here, doubt is not an expression of scepsis it is means for achieving truth. Doubt leads to questioning and questioning leads to reliable knowledge. It is not an empty criticism but a critique of vague or contradictory. It is understanding and not disproof.

Abelard's posthumous influence through his work could not be silenced. He was followed by John of Salisbury, Peter Lombard, Pope Alexander III, Celestine II and Celestine III among others. Due to his innovativeness and anticipation of future philosophy, his work could not be possibly engulfed by his times.

The 12th century is frequently characterised by historians as the *siècle d'essor*, a century of bloom. Why? Rougher mentality was increasingly humanised. Court culture was established, feelings and imagery softened. The Romanesque style was becoming exhausted and Gothic was born. Interest in education increased and the network of schools was getting denser. The most important schools in Bec, Lyon, Montpellier, Reims, Tours, Bologna, Modena, Erfurt, Freising, Cologne and Vienna became predecessors of the first universities. It is also worth mentioning important schools such as the school in Chartres or the school of St. Victor (near Paris). The importance and influence of contact with Byzantine culture and the world of Islam through the Iberian peninsula grew. In abbeys, *scriptoriums* were established (workshops of transcriptions and translations). The translations from Greek and Arabic reached Europe, from Constantinople and Italy, and through Toledo respectively.

Developing liberal arts were an expression of a great thirst for knowledge, however there was also a shift in interests. Ever greater attention was attracted by anthropological and psychological themes and also themes of natural sciences. The interest in cultivation of natural activities grew. Lower manual skills started to be recognised. The scholars returned to antique education with new intensity. Along with the monastic humanism which was personified in Bernard of Clairvaux (1090/1091 1153), we can already talk about a scholastic humanism, which is personified by Alain of Lille (1128 – 1202/1203). Significantly broader literary production of the 12th century was formally still of a better quality. Authors used more metaphors and imagery and they tred to achieve literary elegance and textual perfection.

8. Albertus Magnus and Thomas Aquinas

In the middle of 13th century, so called aristotelian eclecticism prevailed among the scholars. And it is the attempt to overcome it to which the name of Albertus Magnus (1200 – 1280), a member of newly established dominican order and the founder of *studium generale* in Cologne, is related.

The range of his knowledge was so big that he received the attribute "great" from his contemporaries. Albert was trying to create new universal concept of knowledge. He wanted to surpass the eclectic Aristotelianism, he acknowledged the autonomy of profane sciences, their separate subject and method and he released philosophy from its bond to theology. He devoted himself to mineralogy, botany and zoology and he recognised the scientific importance of observation. Albert's work was an expression of the anticipation of renaissance. Despite that however, he never became as important as his student Thomas Aquinas, whom he outlived.

In his work, he fought against the cumbersome and constraining unawareness even if abbots or theologians, who doubted the study of philosophy, were concerned. He claimed that they themselves inhibit the education of others by their incompetence. They were like the gall in the body which intoxicates it, like those who killed Socrates. However Albert did not only criticise but he was also actively disproving of certain opinions. He argued in favour of spherical shape of the Earth by a reference to its round shadow on the Moon during its eclipse. He studied the dependence of atmospheric pressure on the altitude. He laid the foundations for Galilean natural sciences. In his case the vulgar image of the Middle Ages, as a period ungenerous to science, has to be necessarily relativised.

Albert was convinced that human intellect is *divinised* by cultivating philosophy. However, he did not agree with Thomas on certain opinions. His work probably has the greatest significance in the field of anthropology, where he put stress on the physical nature of man which brought him to a new reconsideration of gnoseology. Many consider him to be a predecessor of evolutionism because of his dynamic perception of universe.

The significance of the Dominican Thomas Aquinas (1224/1225 – 1274) for scholastics can be preliminarily justified in three different ways: By the scope and syntheticity of his work, by his profundity and consistency, and by his work's influence which it is still relevant today.

How did Thomas understand the relationship of philosophy and theology? We could say that the core of his work is metaphysics and he is one of the authors who largely contributed to the autonomous position of philosophy in relation to theology. In the introduction to his script *Summa contra Gentiles* (Summa against Gentiles) he writes that "to know everything that intellect can examine about God, a lot of knowledge is necessary, so almost the whole philosophical thinking is focused on understanding God". Therefore, even philosophy is theocentric and it has to be engaged in favour of the cognizability of God. At the same time, theology depends on the philosophical argumentation. This brings Aquinas to a definition of their mutual positions according to their subjects and methods. While theology is higher than philosophy regarding its subject, in terms of its method, philosophy is an autarkic science superior to theology which is methodologically subaltern. Theology builds on principles which are not its own – however they are obvious and accepted from outside. These opinions led to criticism from a so-called new Franciscan school. A script of Franciscan William de la Mare (+1285) *Correctorium fratris Thomae* which disproved 118 theses of Thomas was obligatory study material for Franciscans.

Thomas' work is directed by the quest for objective knowledge, for *adequatio ad rem*. He considers creation of the entities, including the cognizing and cognized to be the basis of objectivity. As created, the cognized becomes the measure of all cognition by created. The ontological independence of the cognized from cognizing is given by their Creator. In his understanding, thinking is the highest form of motion. Intellect is both active and passive (it illuminates so called phantasms and it extracts an intelligible basis from them by abstraction). The active intellect itself is a world in which we cognize. It is a mysterious ability which calls for a broader notion of abstraction. In this sense, Thomas is close to Husserl's perception of essences. Cognition cannot be metaphorically understood as reflection but as an activity, as an active movement of intellect towards a thing without touching it. This obliges and forces man to be humble, to live in a certain way which makes us able to acquire knowledge.

According to Thomas, all entities with the exception of man perceive reality in their own way. Thanks to the soul or intellect, only man is capable of objective knowledge. Everything is just what it is through its *quidditas* and only the soul can be everything through knowledge. Philosophy cannot serve theology anymore, only reality.

Thomas surpasses his teacher Albertus Magnus in anthropology as well. Its basis is an idea of the 'createdness' of the world, which has two aspects: *contingency* and *autonomy*. At the same time, the idea of createdness refers to sustaining the created in existence and also to allowing autonomy and separateness of the created. However, by autonomy, Thomas accentuates more than contingency. Hermeneutic principle, which serves as his basis, is an idea that every entity contains a principle of its own activity. All entities accept effects of other entities according to their own way and nature. Therefore the more perfect the way of existence according to its own essences, the more specific and autonomous the activities of entities will be. Man is endowed with greatest autonomy. Therefore in man the autonomy manifests itself most fully in the order of the created world.

Thomas abandoned the dualism of body and soul. By his concept of spiritual soul, he surpassed Aristotelianism and Albert as well. For Thomas, man became a person which is unique unity in itself. While before Thomas, Christian scholars believed that soul can be understood as a substance separable from body, Thomas comes to the acknowledgement of an essential unity of body and unique rational spirit. Man contributes to all stages of being but at the same time he transcends them. All layers are present in him. According to Thomas, even animal has memory; however man has its higher form (*memoria* vs. *reminiscentia*). Man and higher animals both have sensory perception which is basis of the highest form of knowledge – *intelligere*.

It was said that the basic theme for Thomas was *metaphysics*. With respect to gnoseology, he claims that the very first cognitive act of intellect is knowledge of being (first notion is a notion of being) which becomes the condition of every other knowledge. It is an inevitable subjective gnoseological precondition, primary intuitive conceiving of being which is elaborated by metaphysics only later. What is important is not the chronological order but the fact that in every single act of knowledge, intellect always realises being or existence of things as a precondition of knowledge first. According to Aristotle, this would be the highest, so called third abstraction, however according to Thomas the conceiving of being is not the pinnacle but, on the contrary, it is the beginning. It is *simplex apprehensio*, immediate, intuitive and non-reflected conceiving. Therefore, according to Thomas, metaphysical horizons opens to man with the first action of his intellect. In his script "*Questiones disputatae de veritate*" he says that man experiences immediate evidence of knowledge of existing which is the basis of certainty and evidence of all knowledge. The certainty of intuitive conceiving of existing is based on the certainty of one's own existence. "Through act of thinking, every man assures himself about his own existence, because when he thinks, he has to nod to his existence."

If we understand scientism as definability (subsumption under a higher notion; subsumption of specific notion under a generic notion) then metaphysics must have a different nature than disciplines of *quadrivium*. The *notion of being* cannot be subsumed and therefore it cannot be defined because it is more general than genus. It does not appertain to all entities in the same way and we can also recognise its transcendental specifications, qualities which permeate every entity accompany being like its shadow.

For Thomas, substance is a way of being through itself and in itself. Accident is an entity through something different. He distinguishes *composite substances* which are compositions of matter and form and *simple substances* which are pure forms. He also distinguishes two types of forms: *inherent* (related to matter) and *subsistent* forms (identical to spiritual beings).

The distinction between matter and form has to result from a distinction between the first and the second substance. The first substance is all the particularities and the second is what is involved in multiple individualities/particularities as identic. According to Thomas (contrary to Aristotle), the principle of individuation is matter which he considers to be a passive principle whereas form is an active principle.

Similarly to Aristotle, Thomas distinguishes between *materia prima* and *secunda*. The firs matter is the least perfect form of being, close to nothingness, passive matter itself. *Materia secunda* is a matter which already has a form and is being shaped by it. Matter is a principle of quantitativeness (individualisation) and form is a principle of unification and coalescence. The cause of each thing as a thing however is just form. Matter is determined by its disposability.

The distinction between potency (possibility) and realisation (act) is related to the understanding of causality and metaphysical motion. Thomas ontologically elaborated these basic distinctions: Pure act– *actus purus*, God, is opposite to first matter. All other entities have to be a mixture of possibility and actuality.

The most important notions are the notions of essence and being. According to Thomas, essence is not just this, through which something has being but most of all; it is what defines general being. Entity is established by defining being through essence. The notions "entity", "essence" and "being" are basic inner constitutive principles of everything. Being is simple and one. Its relation to essence is similar as the relation of act and possibility. It is a real difference, so called *distinctio realis*. According to Thomas, the being of essence is ontologically superior which led to his large criticism. Being as *esse commune* does not exist independently, it is just a formal cause of really existing entities. *Esse commune* is less perfect than pure God's being. According to Thomas, God gives more perfection to entities through the act of being than through essence.

In his *Summa Theologica*, Thomas elaborated several so called a posteriori proofs of God's existence, which assume distinction of metaphysical and cosmological levels. These were thought paths of reflection from the intuitive notion of being through essence to the existence of "something" in which essence and being are identical. Based on analogy, "being itself" becomes a derived name of God. (1) The first proof is a proof based on motion, (2) the second one is based on causality, (3) the third on the distinction between inevitability and possibility, (4) the fourth way is an argument based on the degree of ontological nobility and grades of being and lastly (5) the fifth way is an argument based on the purposefulness, teleological structure of existence.

Used and Recommended Literature

Abelard Pierre: Sic et Non (translated by W. J. Lewis (aided by the helpful comments and suggestions of S. Barney) from the Latin text in the critical edition of Sic et Non edited by Blanche B. Boyer and Richard McKeon (University of Chicago Press, 1976).

Anselm of Canterbury: Complete Philosophical and Theological Treatises (Translated by Jasper Hopkins and Herbert Richardson). Minneapolis: The Arthur J. Banning Press, 2000.

Boethius: The Consolation of Philosophy (Translated by David R. Slavitt). Cambridge – London: Harvard University Press, 2008.

Boethius: The Principles of Music (translation by Calvin Martin Bower). George Peabody College for Teachers, 1967.

Brown, Stephen F. – Flores, Juan Carlos: Historica Dictionary of Medieval Philosophy and Theology.. Plymouth: The Scarecrow Press, 2007.

Copleston Frederick: A History of Philosophy. II. New York: Doubleday, 1993.

Dionysius the Areopagite: On the Divine Names and the Mystical Theology (Translated by C.E. Rolt). Grand Rapids, MI: Christian Classics Ethereal Library, 1920.

Eriugena John Scotus: The Division of Nature (translated by I. P.. Sheldon-Williams, revised by John O'Meara). Washington, DC, and Montreal: Dumbarton Oaks and Editions Bellarmin, 1987.

Heinzmann Richard: Olomouc: Štredověká filosofie. 2000.
Kenny Anthony: Medieval Philosophy. Oxford: Clarendon Press, 2007.
Lagerlund Henrik (ed.): Encyclopedia of Medieval Philosophy. Philosophy between 500 and 1500. Springer, 2011.
Leonardi Claudio: Štředověká latinská literatura (6. – 15. století). Praha: Academia, 2014.
Libera de, Alain: Středověká filosofie. Praha: Oikoymenh, 2005.
Luscombe David: Medieval Thought. Oxford: Oxford University Press, 1997.
Marenborn John: Medieval Philosophy. An Historical and Philosophical Introduction. London: Routledge, 2007.
McGrade, A. S. (ed): The Cambridge Companion to Medieval Philosophy. Cambridge: Cambridge University Press, 2006.
Pieper Josef: Scholastika. Praha: ČKA, 1993
Ruud Jay: Encyclopedia of Medieval Literature. Facts on File, 2006.

Doc. Ladislav Tkáčik, PhD.

works as a associated professor at the Department of Philosophy, Faculty of Philosophy and Arts at Trnava University in Trnava, Slovakia. Her main areas of specialization are the Philosophy of Culture, Phenomenology, Philosophical Hermeneutics and Medieval Philosophy. He published a book on the phenomenology of giveness, *Contribution of Emmanuel Lévinas to the Phenomenology of the Gift* (2014), and is a co-author of the book *Vivat, crescat, floreat...* Universitas Tyrnaviensis (2013).

Európska únia
Európsky sociálny fond

Európska únia

Operačný program
VZDELÁVANIE

VÝSKUMNÁ AGENTÚRA